SUPERCONSCIOUS
MEDITATION

SUPERCONSCIOUS MEDITATION

Justin O'Brien
Swami Jaidev Bharati

FULL
CIRCLE

SUPERCONSCIOUS MEDITATION

Copyright © Justin O'Brien (Swami Jaidev Bharati) 2010
First Paperback Edition, 2010
ISBN 978-81-7621-199-4

Published by arrangement with
Yes International Publishers, USA.

 Published by **FULL CIRCLE** *PUBLISHING*
J-40, Jorbagh Lane, New Delhi-110003
Tel: 24620063, 24621011 • Fax: 24645795
E-mail: contact@fullcirclebooks.in • *website:* www.fullcirclebooks.in

Typesetting: SCANSET
J-40, Jorbagh Lane, New Delhi-110003

Printed at Tan Prints (India) Pvt. Ltd., Distt. Jhajjar, Haryana

PRINTED IN INDIA

10/10/01/10/21/SCANSET/DE/TP/TP/NP175/NP175

To

my master,

Swami Rama,

the only man

I ever met

who wanted

utterly nothing for himself

except

another's happiness.

Table of Contents

Introduction

An Open Notice
to One who Wants to Learn Meditation

Among the many interests that engage society today, one of the least worth bothering about appears to be learning to meditate. Or so it seems. It's not that meditation gets bad press; it's rather that meditation doesn't fit readily into our commercially-oriented culture. People simply don't know what's it all about, and so, most hardly care to learn.

Our minds normally are occupied with external events, required tasks, things to remember. Mostly work and play. We get to know ourselves pretty much by engaging the local scene that preoccupies our keen attention. Our interests are groomed to the world at large.

In the face of those engaging occupations, meditation proposes to reverse the direction of our constant attention from the outside world to the world within. My meditation teacher, Swami Rama of the Himalayas, often referred to us as citizens of two worlds – the outer and the inner. Most of us, however, never really get familiar with the advantages of the inner world, and thus its treasures go undiscovered. In fact, if we knew about them from personal experience, many of the vexing problems of our daily life would diminish.

So we need to learn how to meditate. The way to begin is easy, and the entire method is subtle but painless. Keep in mind that haste and harshness have no place in the process. There is no competition with anyone, least yourself. Your involvement is strictly with managing your own act of inner awareness. You will be simply directing your attention in a specific way and noting the results. You stay calmly in charge. Whatever distractions and discomfort you may feel are quite normal at the beginning stage and not the fault of either you or the method. You will go through an adjustment period.

In learning from my Olympian coach, I made all kinds of slips and blunders and still managed eventually to "get it." With this method, one has to work hard to fail.

The whole thrust of meditation is to gain entrance to and fathom all the levels of the mind and thereby gradually discover the wellspring of consciousness from which flows our talents, creativity, wisdom, and sense of immortality. The understanding of our two-fold citizenship builds a bridge that connects both worlds so that we can increase our freedom to conduct our lives in an intelligent, peaceful, and creative manner. The entire inner trip expands self-discovery.

Little did I know what was in store for me when I walked into Swami Rama's house in the Chicago suburbs thirty-five years ago. The morning appointment was for a visit; I thought I would case him out. Instead, he cased me out, and without any fanfare ushered me into his tradition of sages by a formal initiation.

I did not expect that surprise. In the customary centuries-old manner, he whispered a special sound in my ear. In some mysterious way, the repetition of this ancient sound would awaken certain qualities in my character and lure me increasingly into a state of inner silence. In other words, the seed was now germinated; it was up to me to water it continually. A testable self-transformation would eventuate. Leaving his presence somewhat nonplussed, I was to return a few days later at his invitation to learn from him how to meditate.

He sure didn't waste time. I hardly got my coat off when he urged me to sit down and begin. Some minutes later he had infused me with the classical yogic method of meditation. He promised that he would do half the work as long as I showed up and did the practice.

Instantly, my mind posed the question, "How can he do that?" But then he floored me: "I am giving you permission to be the first to teach this ancient method called Superconscious Meditation. Go out and teach others in the world."

My mind reeled with a litany of objections to my

inadequacy, but when I finally settled down from whining inside, I knew that he knew what he was doing, so I had better get used to the task. Besides, how does one say no to a wizard? And so began the never-ending adventure of meditation.

May I just remind you that as you get to know yourself through meditation from the inside out, any fears, lingering hesitations about life, anxieties, and biases you may have will gradually pale so that you can make unbiased choices in your career and life. Obviously these disclosures can't occur over a weekend. But that's what makes the inner journey so interesting!

Justin O'Brien, Ph.D.
Swami Jaidev Bharati

The Art
of the
Inner Journey

In a society that emphasizes enterprising activities and commercial endeavors, meditation can be intimidating. It absents itself from the ordinary utilitarian concerns. The pursued values and actions that establish the work-a-day world are put aside, while the meditator steps away from occupations and worldly duties. The same mind, however, that is deployed for advancing career and raising a family is now used in a totally other direction.

In meditation the mind dwells upon itself in silence, eschewing thought. Little in Western education has prepared us for this kind of self-study. Yet many episodes in the past have given clues to the mind's enthralled experience with its own abilities to be a knowing power. A lot of patience is required of the new meditator.

Leaving aside specific desires and everyday actions that keep one engaged with the everyday world, the meditator examines the mind in itself as a knowing agent. Self-reflection then easily reveals that each day one's mind enters into three distinct states. One is awake, in the very state of mind that pervades most of our day. Retiring at night puts us into two other mind states: a dream realm and a sleep realm. These three states of consciousness constitute our normal existence. Where does meditation fit in? It boldly proposes that, contrary to ordinary expectations, our consciousness is more than the three states of mind, and this inner journey is the way to prove it.

Gazes that Renew and Transcend

In their examination of the totality of human consciousness, the yogic sages – those women and men who have walked their paths to the fullest self-discovery – learned, as we can, two cognitive arts that revive and expand self-awareness beyond the mind's three states. These ancient practitioners bequeathed to humankind two definitive arts, contemplation and meditation, that enable the initiated to achieve the palm of life.

We banter these words "meditation" and "contemplation" around without realizing their profundity. Yet each is a path, a self-conscious discipline, that enables one to pass beyond the borders of rationality into the unknown realm of human trans-consciousness where, according to our ancient travelers, the ultimate treasures of human existence reside.

Thus, the sages pose a new challenge: from where do the ordinary three states of waking, dreaming, and sleeping arise? Is the range of human consciousness composed entirely by borders? Since society is more the product of rational reflection than any other mental state, does that fact make rational awareness the ultimate best one can do?

In admonitions, myths, and enticing stories, various ancient texts narrate the possibilities for attaining, as Plato put it, "the sacred wisdom of the gods." In comparison with the cognitive experience of this knowledge, which we call superconsciousness, the heights of rational discourse – with all its Nobel prizes, its awesome scientific progress, and its artistic accomplishments – are but a sorely dimmed foretaste of the immense bliss and incomprehensible vision that awaits contemplators and meditators.

The sages invite us onto their plane of being, not by struggling after a humanitarian award, nor by disdaining rational endeavors, but by pursuing the very energy that animates our bodies, inspires our highest goals, and gives zest to our actions. The meditator seeks no less than the fountainhead of life and being, the knowledge, as the Upanishads remark, that once tasted makes one immortal.

Besides the marvels of rational analysis, the sages remind us that there lies hidden within us another way to embrace reality, the *unio mystica*, mystical union in enlightenment.

Emmanuel Swedenborg, that 18th century inner traveler extraordinaire, having exhausted his rational interests in the scientific world of his time after having written on virtually every science and craft of his day, finally turned inward in his insatiable quest for the meaning of life itself.

His outward contemplative foray into the vast sciences of the cosmos led him finally to the inner threshold of meditation, where his journey blossomed.

Swedenborg's meditative aspiration came to fruition where, he informs us,

"I was elevated into that light interiorly by degrees, and in proportion as I was elevated, my understanding was enlightened, 'til I was at length able to perceive things which I did not perceive before, and, finally, such things as I could not even comprehend by thought from rational light."

Before explicating the path of meditation, let us examine briefly its favorite companion, called contemplation.

Contemplation

First, a story. While working in England, I met a nurse who worked in the terminal ward of a large London hospital for nearly two decades. Her tenure was almost legendary; rarely did nurses contract for more than five years in this stressful and emotional work. Constantly surrounded by physical and emotional forms of hopeless disintegration, her demeanor, surprisingly, showed a sensitive calmness regarding her occupation. On one visit over tea, I asked her how she coped daily within an environment where anger, fear, despair, and death relentlessly prevailed. She replied that some years earlier she had purchased a cozy cottage in one of those picturesque English country villages outside the city. Most weekends would find her sitting in its garden, facing the westerly landscape, where her sunlit companions grew and blossomed all about, and listening while the season's sounds breezed through the surrounding forest. In the solitary enchantment of those hours, she gazed upon her Brig o' Doon where time retires and the living forces of nature reveal their beauty. She experienced the vision that renews. Glimmers of superconsciousness stirred in her soul and brought her back to work restored.

Reach back into your memory to that special autumn walk some time ago. Recall that stroll through the woods where you were enthralled with the colors shimmering around you in the cool wind while the fallen, rustling leaves scattered as your feet kicked delightfully at them. Remember plodding along the snow-filled sidewalks as the falling white flakes slowly landed on you in the night's stillness. Return to the sandy beach you walked along and the joy of sailing in the sunshine on the deep blue of Lake Superior. Perhaps there have been other solitary moments that you would not have traded for anything else.

How different are those moments from the compelling actions of hurry and worry, the impatient wait for traffic lights to alter, the tense search for the shortest line at the grocery counters, the implacable voice of the boss barking out additional labors for your weary energies.

There was nothing prearranged about your nature walks, no effort at control. There was no need to reason seriously about the situation. You just came along unannounced and were unexpectedly ushered into a higher sense of awareness. Involved with reality, not by intervening into the course of life, but simply by quietly noticing, a revelation occurred. You simply gazed.

Intangible but real, the truth of nature's beauty shows herself to those who are ready. In that enduring exposure, you awakened more. How intangible, almost impractical, this conscious, physical delight in nature's season! Effortlessly, it charms your attention. Bearing that experience you cannot depart from the woods, the snow, the sand, the sea, feeling the same as before.

When you listen to a Mozart concerto, peer at the secrets and beauty of Rembrandt's portraits, read a favorite poem, become transfixed by the shuttling, multicolorful sweep of the aurora borealis in the evening northern sky, the conscious awareness experiences, as James Joyce calls it, an "aesthetic arrest." Your attention is enthralled by a beautifying knowledge that moves your soul to recognize sublimity. More than just mundane moments of physical attraction, your contemplative experience briefly depicts the irresistible radiance of transcendence in the field of time.

Some days you pause amid your busy schedule and ponder a topic in the quiet of your mind, and suddenly, after persistent reflection, a new inference emerges as an unexpected gift. You behold the issue in a new light, and for those brief seconds the march of time halts. Your attention is willingly widened, lifted from its routine cares.

You savor the encounter. Circumstances have evoked an echo within that obliges you to be still.

Human consciousness – in addition to its everyday exertion of reasoning to earn a living, pay bills, and pursue dozens of mental activities – possesses this innate capacity of simply sustaining its gaze in a conscious embrace of beauty and truth. *Contemplatio,* as the Western ancients referred to it, is this experience from which our modern word contemplation evolved.

More than mere general perception, the art of contemplation implies a certain kind of predisposition, more along the lines of fostering a condition of ready watchfulness or perspicacity. As a vessel of awareness you are using your mind and senses not as inertly peering into space, as it were, but sustaining a conscious alertness of the object of your interest.

The act of discerning springtime's emerging jack-in-the-pulpit produces a special connection between the agent of awareness and the spring reality. Awareness engages its revealing target. A union ensues between knower and flower. Two life forces meet and pure knowledge convenes. Contemplation unfolds a little more of the truth of one's own self as well as that of the universe.

Meditation

The versatility of your mind shares yet another route to transcendence – that of meditation – when it is sufficiently invited to do so. To examine its dynamics, let us set up the context in which most citizens find themselves: the busy metropolitan life of a city. Enjoying life's abundance as we are, eventually we are forced to deal with obsolescence. Businesses start up and close. Household articles lose their use over time because they wear out. Winter succeeds autumn. Clinging to your children defeats love. Our daily efforts with material things produce eventual entropy. We buy, consume, and begin anew. If we don't understand this world and its inexorable ways, we head for heartache. It's part of what the sages call chasing the delusions of life.

> Lead me from the unreal to the real.
>
> *Brihadaranyka Upanishad*

Instead of being monopolized by the world about you, your mind can turn about and withdraw into its primal source of life and light. Without moving the body, you can embark to the inner galaxies of memory, creativity, and beyond.

For some accustomed to being continuously preoccupied, meditation can be a shock. A strange reversal of mind occurs, spontaneously, when we close off our senses to the outside world, quiet down, and systematically slip into the stream of our consciousness. There is no weariness inside. In our ordinary world of diminishing returns, the mind is unique: a self-renewing reality. The mind, unlike matter, doesn't diminish with use, but instead, by this inner dwelling, the mind increases its power of refreshment that affects even its body.

The gaze inward is full of surprises. Although our eyes are closed, we still look upon the horizon of our minds and become aware of their active inhabitants: feelings, images, ideas, and their variations. But our excursion within is not merely to take an inventory; rather it searches out the life source within that enables us to have those occupants in the first place. We want to find that fountain of peace, love, and truth that occasionally emits hints of its presence. We want to know our soul in its pristine existence. Cast among all the roles we've already played in life, up comes that irrepressible question: "Who am I really?"

The bewildering mystery of meditation is that sitting quietly over time can bring about the stupendous marvel of disclosure that we seek. Thus, asking whether or not to investigate meditation is really asking the question, "How free do I want to become?"

How
to
Meditate

Welcome to your inward journey. In our ancient tradition of meditation, we place an emphasis on getting the aspirant into the practical dynamics of the method at the very beginning. In other words: how to do it is right up front. The idea is "less theory, more practice." With the experience of some actual practice, the explanation of the theory is then more easily understood.

We want to initiate the early practice of the art of meditation so that from this experiential groundwork the understanding of its philosophy ensues. There is nothing worse than an unmarried marriage counselor! Hence the ancient saying *Prius vita quam doctrinam* fits well: "Get busy doing it first, and then speculate about it." Just reading a menu won't satisfy the hunger.

The secret to meditation is simple: do the steps in sequence. This ancient, systematic procedure moves your awareness from the gross level to the subtle. There is no shortcut. Once you have the steps down, the benefits will become self-evident. There are seven sequential steps for meditation; just follow them in numerical order.

We start at the most obvious level: how to take care of your body. Find a comfortable chair; even a recliner will do. Take off your shoes and douse the lights.

Posture

Posture in meditation is extremely important. In posture, you have a choice; either sit on the floor or sit on a chair. If you wish to use a wooden or metal chair, you might consider putting a blanket or pillow on the seat to make it more comfortable. The meditation postures are designed so that you sustain your head, neck, and trunk in an upright position without being rigid. In other words, hold yourself vertically as best as you can.

It may come as a surprise to learn that in the classic meditation manual, *The Yoga Sutras*, the ancient text mentions only that the recommended posture for meditation is one that keeps the practitioner upright in a steady and comfortable manner.

It is unusual that these two simple qualities alone should be cited and nothing else. Strain and any military-like pose is eschewed; meditation is not boot camp. You don't want the discomfort while attempting a rigid stability to distract you from your inward journey. Keep the head up and chest open without slouching or hunching over. Do not bow or bend forward.

Some yoga groups may insist upon certain leg postures without realizing that the spinal column is the crucial part of one's anatomy that needs to be kept upright. We want no undue pressure on the spinal nerves or the circulation of the blood, nor do we want any interference with the motion of the lungs. Where or how you place your legs is not as important as sitting upright and comfortably with or without back support. Given your age and circumstances, sit as straight as your body permits in the most comfortable position.

Two simple poses for meditation are the Friendship Posture or *Maitri Asana,* and the Easy Pose or *Sukhasana.* In the Friendship Posture, the meditator sits on a chair. The feet are flat on the floor, the hands rest on the thighs, and the torso is upright with head, neck, and back straight and erect.

In the Easy Pose, the practitioner sits on the floor. The

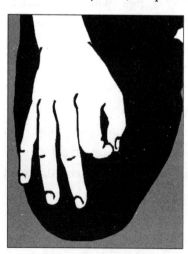

Jnana Mudra

left foot is placed under the right knee, and the right foot is placed under the left knee. This is the common posture for children listening to a story. For more comfort, place a small cushion under the tailbone to help keep the torso erect.

In all meditation postures, your hands should be placed on top of your thighs with the arms relaxed. Lightly press the tips of the index fingers to the tips of the thumbs in a finger lock called *Jnana Mudra*. It keeps the circuit of energy flowing within your body.

For those who are proficient in yoga postures, you may wish to use one of the other two classic meditation postures. They are the Auspicious Posture, *Swastikasana*, and the Accomplished Posture, *Siddhasana*.

The Auspicious Posture is recommended especially for women. Sitting on a pillow or cushion on the floor, bend the left leg and place the bottom of the foot against the inside right thigh. Then bend the right leg and slide the foot up between the left thigh and calf muscles. The big toe should peek out at the top. The toes of the left foot should then be pulled up so that the big toe is visible on that side also.

The Accomplished Posture is recommended especially for men. Also done on the floor with a cushion, this pose keeps the heels and ankle bones aligned. After bending your left leg, place the left heel at the perineum between the anus and the genitals. The right leg is then bent, and the right heel placed at the pubic bone above the genitals. Arrange the ankles so they are lined up or touch each other. As with the Auspicious Posture, the big toes are pulled up to be visible while the other toes are hidden between the thighs and calves.

Often the Lotus Posture, *Padmasana*, is shown as a pose of meditation. In this posture, the feet are turned

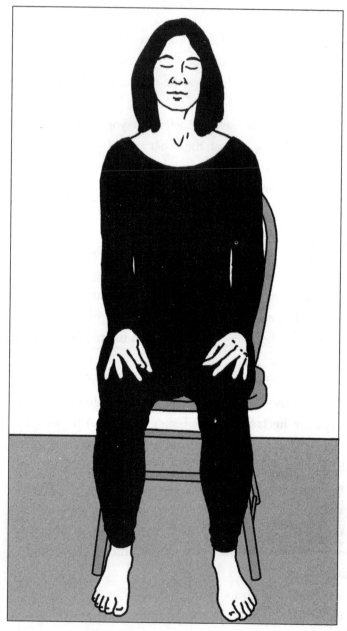

The Friendship Posture, *Maitri Asana*

The Easy Pose, *Sukhasana*

The Auspicious Posture, *Swastikasana*

The Accomplished Posture, *Siddhasana*

upward, lying on the opposite thigh. It is a limbering posture in hatha yoga exercises but is not recommended as a meditation posture. It is difficult to hold properly for meditation and takes many years to perfect. An image of it, however, is often used as a symbol of pure meditation, the union of body, mind, and spirit, both in yoga and Buddhism.

When you choose a meditation posture, practice it regularly, without changing it, until you are very comfortable in it. Getting adjusted to being upright with arms at ease on the thighs, the unmoving body sets the stage for proceeding to the next step of meditation.

Diaphragmatic Breathing

Let's now move on to that most dynamic connection between your mind and body: your breath. The Himalayan Tradition is unique in the importance it gives to the act of breathing. After all, without the breath there is no life, in spite of the finest cuisine and even Perrier water!

Many students might be slightly perturbed to be told by the teacher that they breathe incorrectly. It's been my international experience, however, that most people are poor breathers. It's also my experience that these same people do not grasp the connection between the powers of their mind, their breathing, and their emotions. Here is where meditation steps into the arena of life and shows us how to optimize our breathing and in the process learn to control our thoughts and emotions.

As you read this section, imagine yourself doing the practice of meditation.

You are sitting with your eyes closed and wondering what to do next as all sorts of ideas and images engage your inner attention. Take one hand and place it upon your abdomen just above your navel. That hand will become aware of a slight movement. It is your abdominal wall moving back and forth. You feel the gentle pressure against your palm as the abdomen protrudes slightly forward and then recedes. When you feel the abdominal wall recede toward the spine, know that it is the correct movement for exhalation. When the abdominal wall extends slightly outward, that is the correct movement for inhalation. Allow this action of breathing to continue its course in that manner. The abdomen moves in and out. Don't raise your chest. As you sense your lungs expanding and contracting, keep the emphasis of your breathing near the navel. Instead of lifting your upper chest to breathe, sustain the abdominal or belly motion. Actually, you are feeling the outer reaction of the inner motion of the diaphragmatic muscle moving up and down. Put a little pressure on the exhalation by pressing inward with your abdominal muscles, but do not force the inhalation out. Let your inhalation simply occur; it acts as a rebound.

This manner of breathing, which is the most natural for the human body, may seem awkward at first, but you are actually in the midst of retraining the respiratory system to return to its optimal norm. Watch a baby breathing with its tummy rising and falling, and you will see how natural abdominal breathing is. The benefits will show up almost immediately. When you sit to meditate, do this exchange of exhalation-inhalation with full attention for ten to fifteen strokes.

Breath Awareness

Now shift your attention to the flow of your breath. Sense the breath flow and watch it carefully. This is called breath awareness. It is most important that you now refine your breathing in the following ways.

- Note if there are pauses during the transitions between inhalation and exhalation. Breathe continuously. Allow your exhalation and inhalation to immediately follow each other without any stoppage between them. When you complete your exhalation, your inhalation immediately begins and vice versa.

- Note if you are making any nasal sounds. Breathe, as best you can, without any emitted sounds from throat or nostrils. If there is sound, slow down the pace, let up on the pressure of moving the lungs, or clear the nostrils.

- Keep your breathing as smooth and even as possible.

- In conclusion, you are now breathing deeply, smoothly, continuously, and quietly. Continue guiding your breath for ten to fifteen more sets.

Knowingly or not, you have introduced a profound change into your metabolism. Everything functions in your body in reference to the breath motion. There is no finer way to breathe for health, clarity of mind, and overall wellness than diaphragmatic breathing.

Your attentive breathing integrates and harmonizes the connection between your mind and body, which you feel as a certain rhythm. An emerging sense of serenity is the emotional consequence of proper breathing. As you are voluntarily making each of the breath adjustments, note the results.

You, the meditator, are proving each of the steps as you go through the practice!

Progressive Relaxation

Now that you are becoming familiar with the breathing process, the next step toward meditation follows an easy sequence for relaxation. Even though you are fairly relaxed by now due to the breathing practice, a further sequence will reinforce the preparation for the subtler steps. While you continue diaphragmatic breathing throughout the next practice, carefully instigate the following.

- Bring your inner attention to your forehead. Ask your body to release any tensions, like frowning or tightness, that may be in that part of your body. Do the same as you mentally come down your body, taking a full breath at each of the parts. Bring your attention, in sequence, to your
  > eyebrows
  > eyelids
  > cheeks
  > lips
  > jaw
  > neck
  > muscles.
- Now pause and take a deep breath, both exhalation and inhalation.
- Next, bring your attention to the back of your neck and shoulders, releasing any tension.
- Bring your attention down both arms
  > past the elbows
  > past the wrists
  > to the fingertips.
- Pause with a deep breath, exhaling and inhaling as you release any tension.
- Retrace your attention up your arms to your neck and then into the upper chest. Pause with a deep breath.

- Next, be aware of your
                    solar plexus
                    hips
                    pelvic area.
- Pause with a deep inhalation and exhalation.
- Now bring your attention to your
                    thighs
                    knees
                    calf muscles
                    ankles
                    feet and toes.
- You have relaxed the major portions of your body. Now imagine that you can exhale from the top of your head, the crown area, downward through your entire body and out your feet.
- Then inhale from your feet up through your body and out the crown of your head. Feel as though your breath was traveling in those two directions, down and up.
- Continuously imagine breathing the length of your body down and up, up and down, for ten to fifteen breaths.

Sense Withdrawal

You have been breathing down and up with your attention

following your breath as best you can. The groundwork is now in place, and you are ready to proceed to the final segments of the preparation for meditation.

In this next portion of the meditative process, you are gathering your attention away from your body so you can focus fully on something else. You will pull your body attention from the lower levels of your body up through specific areas along the spine (*chakras*) and bring a sense of awareness to a higher point in your body.

Again, follow the sequence as stated below and sustain your breathing as deep, smooth, continuous, and quiet throughout the remaining sequence.

- Breathe from the crown of your head down to your feet.

- Keeping your attention on the movement of your breath, exhale from your head down only to your ankles, ignoring your feet. Then inhale from your ankles up to the crown of your head.

- Next, exhale from your crown down to your knees and inhale from there back up to your crown.

- Now exhale down along your spinal column to the base of your spine and inhale up your spinal column to your crown.

- Next exhale from the crown down to your bladder region, a few inches above the base of your spine. Inhale up to your crown.

- Exhale down along the spinal column to the solar plexus and return back up to the crown.

- Exhale down to the center of the chest, next to the heart, and back up to the crown.

- Next, exhale down to your throat pit and up to your crown.

- Exhale down to the juncture between your two nostrils above the upper lip, the columella, and keep your attention there at that entrance point as you breathe in and out. Feel the cool air coming in and the warm air going out. Stay with this breathing for ten to fifteen breaths.

- Now raise all your attention to the space between your two eyebrows (the *ajna* chakra). Breathe in and out from that point and sustain your attention there.

- As you breathe along with your easy attention gently focused at that space, remind yourself of the following:

  1. You have a body and senses, but you yourself are neither the body nor the senses. They are your gross tools.

  2. You have a rational mind and a thinking power, but you are neither the mind nor the thinking power. They are your finer tools.

  3. Further within you resides your real nature: a nature full of peace, bliss, and wisdom. You are now entering

into the silence which sets up the conditions for that pure nature to unfold into your life.

Concentration

As the weeks go by, your posture will gradually assume a steady stability, and it will be easier to concentrate. With gentle attention focused at the space between your eyebrows and fostering an ease of breathing, your job now is just to concentrate, allowing for the stream of consciousness to pass before your mind's eye. Just notice, without taking any concern, whatever ideas or images emerge.

Settle into remaining still and attentive at the space between both eyebrows. It is the steady awareness that forms this step; awareness without chasing after any ideas or images. Remain uninterested in the stream of consciousness that parades before your mind.

You may be surprised at the number and kinds of ideas and images that will arise in your inner awareness, but it does not matter what comes up. Your task is to remain a witness to the entire entourage.

Meditation

As you gain competency in staying your attention, the power of your concentration will perdure into meditation. Thus, the final step is to expand beyond your rational mind and enter into its supernatural fountainhead of unalloyed peace, bliss, and wisdom. The path of meditation has a staggering climax. In that experience you will live your life from the absolute freedom of your own immortal nature.

The mind, however, does not like to give up its dependence upon treasured ideas. We are quite possessive of them, especially since they enable us to earn a living and promote our daily welfare. The act of meditation takes head-on the mind's tenacious hold upon its memories and releases our dependence upon them. This does not imply an empty state of mind. Rather, unknown to the beginning meditator, a transpersonal field of knowledge awaits discovery.

To assist the meditator's reliquishment of the mind's possessions, the sages often gave special sounds or visual forms to their students to steady the mind as well as elevate its abilities in order to proceed past them. The Himalayan Tradition prefers to render a special sound *(mantra)* to the student since this tool is easier to assimilate as an object of attention.

Beginners may use the universal mantra *So-Hum*. It is a Sanskrit word meaning, "I am that." I am not what I think I am, but the great unknown for which I strive. I am not my thoughts; I am not my feelings; I am that power of consciousness.

These two syllables, then, will support and sustain your focus on being an attentive observer rather than being involved in your thinking process. The liberating function of the mantra relieves the mind of distractive ideas, images, and sense impressions that impede inner progress.

When using the mantra, wait until you feel settled into the rhythm of your breath. Wait until the train of ideas slows down. Then simply listen to the sound *So-Hum* in your memory. As you inhale, remember the sound *So;* as you exhale, remember the sound *Hum*. Hear the sounds and align the sounds with the cycle of breathing. This mantra adjunct will help keep you centered in the silence within. When you notice your mind drift off into a train of thought, simply refocus your attention upon your breath and the mantra sound and go deeper inside.

Here is what the entire sequence of connective steps for meditation looks like:

1. Posture

2. Diaphragmatic Breathing

3. Breath Awareness

4. Progressive Relaxation

5. Sense Withdrawal

6. Concentration

7. Centering Through Witnessing:
   the flow of meditation with a mantra

These steps are all that are needed to meditate. Simple! Within a short time you will have memorized the entire sequence. Early benefits will arrive within days. Usually a notable calming effect will become apparent. Some of the stressful status of your body will fade away; even your blood pressure will seek to normalize.

Begin your journey with ten to fifteen minutes. Don't push. Practice at least once a day. As you become familiar with meditation, your stay will naturally lengthen.

But there is much more to learn, much more to achieve in meditation. This is only the beginning. Like the salesman who entered a taxi at LaGuardia Airport and asked the driver how to get to Carnegie Hall, the reply came back: "Practice, practice!"

An
Interlude
with
Breath

It almost goes without saying that the easiest entrance into the art of meditation is by regulating the breath. We learn that with practice. But then one wonders exactly what is so important about breathing. After all, we associate common sense with breathing, so why bother anymore about it?

Aside from breathing's indispensable function of keeping the body alive – just tally how long you can continue reading without inhaling – the breath offers more than the subtle responsibility of keeping body and mind coordinated. Any doubts on this matter can be resolved by observing what happens to your ability to stay focused when you inadvertently breathe in a haphazard manner. Just recall how serene you felt when you huffed and puffed using your upper chest!

Proper breathing has become a lost art. By not taking breathing seriously, its potential benefits are lost. The fact that breathing continues on its own without calling attention to itself does not imply that breathing is functioning for optimum physical and mental health. In most cases, the opposite is true. Proper breathing is essential for progress in meditation.

Let's take a closer look at the body's design for breathing. The average adult breathes about 26,000 times a day, that is, 18 times a minute. Your chest houses your remarkable lungs, the essential organs of respiration. These two spongy masses of tissue extend from just above the clavicle bones down to the diaphragm floor. Together, they fill out the width and height of your thoracic cavity. They are wider in their lower halves than at their tops. Deep fissures divide each lung into lobes; the shorter and broader right lung contains three lobes, while the left lung contains two lobes with the heart nestling in its indention.

The light, porous texture of the lungs is extremely elastic; hence their capacity for inflation and deflation. The structural connections that allow the air to enter the lungs from the mouth or nose resemble an upside-down tree. The trunk of the tree is your windpipe, or trachea, which extends from the larynx in the throat downward through the chest. The trachea branches out into the lungs, dividing into bronchi, three for the right lobes and two for the left lobes. These bronchi divide again into smaller branches called bronchioles, which sprout the leaves of the tree, the alveoli. In these terminal sites the actual exchange of air and blood takes place.

When we breathe, air enters through our nose or mouth, descending through the windpipe into the far reaches of the alveoli. There the inflation and deflation of the tiny air sacs diffuse new air into the bloodstream, exchanging it for the old air. Both airs are rapidly transported throughout the body via the blood by the heart's incessant squeezing movements. The heart sends its venous blood to the lungs to be freshly oxygenated and simultaneously sends the newly rejuvenated blood received from the lungs to the heart, which sends a fresh supply of oxygen to all the body's capillaries. This cycle repeats itself thousands of

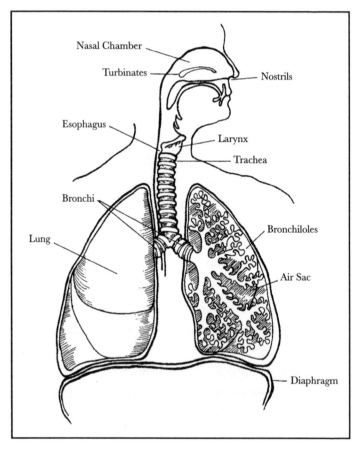

Respiratory System

times throughout the day. The bronchial tree services the body with ever-fresh air at inspiration and receives the used carbon dioxide from the venous blood for expiration.

The lungs themselves are basically passive. They cannot expand or compress on their own. They need the assistance of the muscles alongside the ribcage, those of the abdominal region, and especially the diaphragm. The diaphragm is the curved sheath of muscle, acting like a moveable floor-ceiling, separating the lungs and heart from the lower organs.

The combined pressure of these three muscle areas against the lungs causes the exchange of gases by the lungs. Humans can breathe by any one of three different ways: chest breathing, clavicular breathing, and diaphragmatic breathing.

Chest breathing moves the air into the lungs by expanding the upper chest. It fills the middle and upper portion of the lungs while minimizing use of the larger, lower lobes. Since this breathing requires deliberate lifting of the ribcage, often seen in a military posture, it uses more energy than any other type of breathing and causes the heart to work harder.

Clavicular breathing is used for emergencies, when one is winded or utterly exhausted and needs maximum air. This breathing process demands a great amount of energy to perform and thus is not the normal method of breathing.

Diaphragmatic breathing is the most efficient type of breathing in virtually all circumstances. It employs the maximum use of the diaphragm and is actually the most natural way to breathe. It is the way we breathe when we are unconscious or in deep sleep. Proper diaphragmatic breathing allows the richest exchange of oxygenated blood because most of the alveoli are in the lower portion of the lungs.

In diaphragmatic breathing, the diaphragm relaxes upward, compressing the lungs for exhalation. It then tightens and flattens downward, allowing for the recoil of the lungs and the consequent inhalation of fresh air. This basic motion has far more subtle influences upon your nerves, thoughts, and emotions than you realize. Stress upsets the coordinated motion between the breath, heart, and lungs, but diaphragmatic breathing recovers the balance.

Once you begin to guide your diaphragmatic breathing, the second important modification to good breathing is to pace your breathing cycle into a balanced rhythm. Exhale and inhale with an even distribution of air. A rhythmic exchange of the diaphragm motion allows a one-to-one ratio between exhalation and inhalation.

The principal organ for breathing is your nose, not your mouth. Your nose, together with the connecting internal organs which lead to your windpipe, provides the proper passageway for the air to reach your lungs and for carbon dioxide to be discharged. Your nostrils serve many indispensable purposes for breathing. First, the air rushing over the membranes of the nostrils swirls around to be warmed and moistened before proceeding to the lungs, thus preventing the shock of cold or dry air. Second, the nostril membranes are coated with fine hairs which filter pollution and foreign particles from the air before it enters your lungs. Even before oxygen reaches your brain from your lungs, your nose stimulates brain functions electrically by passing air over your nasal olfactory nerve, which is directly connected to the brain.

The division of your nose into two nostrils focuses your breathing and your energy all day long. Your breath is prominent in one nostril at a time, alternating periodically from one to the other. This is due to the regular swelling and shrinking of erectile tissue in the nostrils. While the tissue in one nostril swells, the air flow is gradually cut off from that nostril and switched to the opposite nostril. Throughout twenty-four hours, your breath predominates alternately in each nostril in concert with the rhythm of your energy.

Most of the time you are probably not aware that your breath is stronger in one nostril, yet in a healthy adult one nostril is predominant for approximately two hours before the flow of air shifts to the other nostril for another two hours. This natural cycle occurs throughout the day unless interfered with by emotional disturbances, lack of rest, irregular eating patterns, sleep, air pollution, or illness.

This fascinating biological rhythm pulsates throughout the human body, affecting every organ and system, from mental alertness to the healing of wounds. We pay little heed to the crucial work of the breath rhythm, even though it modulates the basic rest-activity cycles that comprise our daily lives regardless of our genders or occupations. This rhythm of energy is called the ultradian cycle (from ultradies, meaning many times per day).

Nostril dominance is extremely important in any discussion of stress, but as strange as it sounds, the changing of the cycle of nostril dominance also greatly affects your moods, and, of course, your ability to meditate. Over the centuries, this phenomenon has been studied by yogis, who noted the relationship between the breath flow and its impact upon the body and mind.

Among other facts, they found that when the breathing force of the air is stronger in the right nostril, a person feels more active. The converse also holds true. When the force of air flows predominantly through the left nostril, the person desires more passive, receptive activities. Research has concurred that when the right nostril is dominant, the left hemisphere of the brain is more operative; when air flows dominantly through the left nostril, the right hemisphere of the brain is more operative. The entire body cues up for each change.

Practically speaking, your right nostril governs the dynamic expressions of your energy self. The yogis connected it to the sun because it aids in all active psychological and physiological processes. If one breathes from the right nostril, one feels more energetic, concerned about external work and events. One will also feel physically warmer and sharply aware.

If one breathes from the left nostril, traditionally associated with the moon, the more passive psychological and physiological processes are served. One feels quieter, more concerned with internal thoughts and feelings, intuition, and the physical correlates of thirst and coolness.

Extremes in nostril dominance are also quite possible. Interference in the cycle will prolong the flow in one nostril, leading to imbalance. Prolonged breathing from the right nostril can lead to hyperactivity, while prolonged breathing from the left nostril can lead to sadness and apathy.

The easiest way to shift your energy is to shift your breathing. When you are hyperactive and cannot slow down your thinking and actions, your right nostril will be dominant and your left nostril will be almost totally shut down. When you are depressed or withdrawn, your left nostril will be dominant and your right nostril will be almost totally shut down. To get back in balance, you need to open the air flow in the opposite nostril. Consciously shifting nostril dominance can be accomplished by practicing for ten to fifteen minutes alternate nostril breathing (see page 63). By directed breathing you can effectively reshape the flow of your energy and emotions.

There are moments when both nostrils flow equally.

Usually this brief event occurs during the alteration of dominance from one nostril to another. The subjective feelings then are clarity and poise, with a serene, calm comfort. This middle flow of the breath is the primary doorway to the expansion of consciousness. Deep meditation is possible only when both nostrils are equally flowing. That is why meditation techniques focus on the breathing so insistently, a fact sadly neglected by many meditation methods. By controlling your breath, you are thus able to control and moderate your emotions, physical energy, and mental clarity.

Emotions and Breath

Our emotions produce startling alterations in our breathing patterns. When we get excited, our respiratory rate changes from its previous pattern into one that accompanies the new emotional state. Likewise, when we become sad, our breath rate changes accordingly. It is this unique combination of thought plus emotion plus breath rate that shapes metabolism, the energy of our behavior, and our ability to proceed in meditation.

Uncontrolled emotions often get in the way of better alternatives. It is impossible for us to enter a state of meditation when in an unbalanced frame of mind due to an emotional condition, but the signs and symptoms of an emotional imbalance or disequilibrium are always reflected in our breath. Happily, just as our emotions are mirrored in our breath; our breath is able to calm all our emotions. Knowing this truth gives us a tremendous edge in shaping the powerful energy of our emotions and preparing ourselves for meditation.

The yogis of the Himalayas have shared the results of their breath investigations and concluded that the rhythmic use of the lower lobes, in diaphragmatic breathing, is the expeditious form for balancing the emotions and establishing a meditative mood. Their findings are not radical, but they do second the natural motion of effective breathing dictated by the dynamic functioning of the human respiratory system.

Since the pure method of meditation builds upon our nature, finding the most natural mode of breathing would seem to offer the best results. Thus, for the dedicated meditator, personal awareness attends to the action of breathing. Sitting still and just breathing does not indicate passivity; rather, like a surfer, we ride the waves of our vital breaths, monitoring the flow as it occurs.

Instead of just ignoring the manner of our breathing like we do during most of our day, for meditation we deliberately redesign the flow of our respiratory pattern. We bring our full attention to participate in the exchange of air by exerting management over the flow. We are self-consciously aware of our own involvement in the ongoing dynamics of our breathing.

The symptomatic clues to this dynamic alteration due to breathing are seen, at the corporeal level, in our actual heart rate, blood pressure, immune system, as well as our involuntary muscular contractions – all of which enjoy, over time, an improved homeostatic balance.

At the emotional and mental levels, we gradually experience a sense of mental clarity and calm alertness with a growing confidence to manage our emotions under duress. Hence a systemic impact ensues upon the entire field of our body-mind status when we are aware of our breathing and exert control over it.

Nasal Cleansing

With so much emphasis on breathing, it is evident that the nose is an important piece of equipment and needs to be kept in good working order. Dust, air pollutants, bacteria, viruses, fungi, and food toxins all effect change in the mucus and mucus membranes of the nasal passages. Usually this change is negative, from a stuffy nose to an infection. The mucus keeps these pollutants moving along out the nose, but occasionally there is a breakdown in the system.

Irregular lifestyle habits, dry air, poor food, and extremes of temperature dry out the mucus membranes and make them ineffective. When the mucus membranes are unable to do their cleaning work, the result is a rapid multiplication of the unwelcome elements.

One solution to this problem is the use of the nasal wash, or *jal neti*, used for centuries in many cultures. It involves washing out the nostrils with warm salt water to dissolve dry mucus, clean the mucus membranes, and free the sinus passageways so they can do their best work again. Saline solution is very comfortable to the body; it approximates the composition of our tears. In the nasal wash, a mild saline solution (non-iodized, pure salt) is poured from a spouted vessel into one nostril and then allowed to flow out the other. The procedure is repeated with the opposite nostril.

Regular, preferably daily, use of this practice will make most sinus problems, colds, asthma, and sinus headaches problems of the past. The clean, open nostrils will also prepare the body-mind complex for meditation.

Diaphragmatic Breathing

- Bring your attention to the breathing motion already in progress in the lower region of your chest. Concentrate your attention on the space between your navel and your sternum. Place your right hand there. Let your hand push gently against this part of your anatomy as you exhale and release when you inhale fresh air.

- Place your left hand on your upper chest. You should feel no movement here; your hand should not move with the breath.

- Keep your hands in place and get used to the feeling of the movement for a few minutes. Think of your lower chest as a rubber balloon filling with air and then flattening as the air is released.

- Now put more emphasis on your exhalation, pressing on the space between your navel and your sternum to get rid of the stale air. Do not force fresh air into your lungs at the inhalation. Merely allow the outward motion of your abdomen to occur without effort. Practice this movement for at least twenty breaths.

- When the diaphragmatic movement seems easy and comfortable, bring your attention to the flow of your breath. Just be aware of your breathing and notice the flow. If you sense that the flow is jerky, smooth it out. If you sense the flow is halting or there are long gaps during the breath cycle, allow the flow to be as continuous as possible, exhalation followed by inhalation, one right after the other.

- Finally, have a sense that your breathing is moving towards an even rhythmic exchange. Do not rush the cycle. Allow your mind to coast along with the breath. In this way your breathing and your attention unite for optimum energizing.

According to the Himalayan yogis, there is a hidden facet to our breathing that accounts for vitality. The real, but esoteric, anatomy discerned by these practitioners allowed them to speak of subtler energy factors that underlie our obvious corporeality. They referred to the principal support of our life as *prana*. This Sanskrit word denotes the primary unit of embodied living. We live due to its animating presence in our person. Although undetectable with conventional apparatus, *prana* surrounds and permeates the universe. Thus, all of nature participates in its ambiance. We breathe it constantly. The chemical oxygen serves as the empirical carrier or vehicle that supplies us with this life force. In addition, we derive it subsidiarily from the sun, water, food, ideas, and people.

Since the yogis worked mostly with improving the flow of *prana* in their oxygen, they were keenly alert to the impediments that prevent its efficient utilization. Gradually they developed a series of exercises pertaining to the facilitation of the life force. These exercises were summed up under the term *pranayama* – the methods of controlling and streamlining the absorption of the life force into our life systems.

Breathing Exercises

For enhancing the preparation of meditation, two major examples of yogic *pranayama* have been selected, as they are easily deployed and immediately effective in ridding the body of excessive carbon dioxide. Due to irregular breath patterns throughout our working day, each body becomes overloaded with that toxin, irritating the nervous system, constricting muscles, and inducing fatigue.

During the day, your mind is frequently interrupted.

These momentary interruptions, and the resulting pauses in your breath cycle, allow carbon dioxide to accumulate in your body. Carbon dioxide irritates your nervous system and produces a general feeling of fatigue in your body and distraction in your mind. Yogic breath exercises are powerful practices designed to remove toxins and restore metabolic balance.

The first exercise, *nadi shodhana,* is commonly called channel purification or alternate nostril breathing. We want to expedite the cleansing of carbon dioxide from the lungs, and this is a gentle, subtle method.

When you have been working hard, you may accumulate stressful feelings that distort your judgment and make you tense. Rebalancing emotional energy and clearing the mind is important for your performance. One of the easiest ways to clear and balance your system and regain a sense of self-control over your energies is through alternate nostril breathing. By directing the flow of your breath alternately in each nostril, you allow thought, emotion, and the autonomic nervous system to establish their synchronistic relationship, forming a self-directing center in your energy.

* Sit comfortably with your head, neck, and trunk erect. Keep both feet flat on the floor. Close your mouth and your eyes. Begin focusing your attention on your diaphragmatic breathing. Breathe for five complete breaths.

- Bend your index and middle fingers of the right hand to touch the palm. This is called the *Vishnu mudra*.

- Bring that hand up to your nose and gently press your thumb against the side of the right nostril while exhaling through the left nostril. As you complete your exhalation, gently close your left nostril with your ring finger, simultaneously releasing your thumb to open the right nostril. Inhale slowly through the right nostril.

- Repeat the process from the beginning twice more.

- While using *Vishnu mudra*, keep your palm away from the face so that the breath can move freely.

- After your third inhalation, do not close the right nostril. Keep it open and immediately exhale slowly from it while holding the left nostril closed.

- Then open the left nostril for the inhalation while closing the right nostril. Repeat this procedure twice more.

- Bring your hand away and breathe diaphragmatically through both nostrils for three breaths.

- Repeat the entire sequence once more.

At first, the switching of the nostrils may seem awkward. With practice, however, this movement becomes smoother and easier. For some time your exhalation may be longer or shorter than your inhalation. As you become more

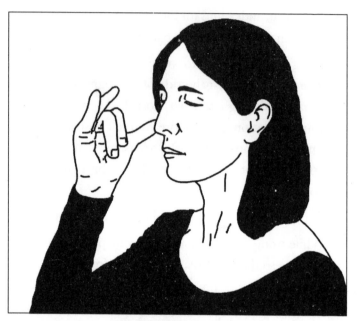

Alternate Nostril Breathing

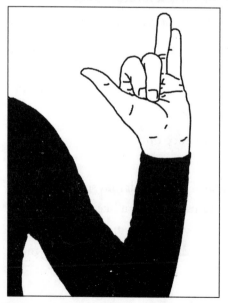

Vishnu Mudra

comfortable with the practice, guide your breathing so that your exhalation-inhalation cycles become more even and balanced. Remember, the diaphragm does the work; allow the breath exchange to be guided by the movement of the diaphragm. Do not aimlessly manipulate your nostrils but concentrate carefully on feeling the flow of the breath. Remember, like any other art, breathing skill comes with practice. Some key points:

- Keep the sphincter muscles contracted throughout.
- Adjust the flow of the breath so that it is approximately even in duration as well as steady.
- Change nostrils in a comfortable, smooth, slow exchange.
- Over time, the inhalations and exhalations can be lengthened in duration, provided one stays comfortable. This is not, however, an endurance contest in breath exchange.
- Yogis prefer to begin exhalation on the left side during the day, and the right side at night. The careful regulation of alternate nostril breathing has a stabilizing effect upon the emotions. One's mood tends to return to a more balanced outlook after its use.

The second exercise, *kapalabhati*, or forced exhalation, emphasizes an expulsion of air by vigorously forcing the abdominal muscles to press quickly backwards toward the spine. Imagine that you were pushing your navel backward in one quick stroke and then immediately releasing the pressure in order to inhale. Sitting in an upright posture, this breathing is done through the nostrils, but all attention is focused on the quick backwards jerk of the abdominal region. Inhalation is a spontaneous rebound as the tightened pressure is released.

Since the movement is done in rapid succession, the practitioner can gradually increase the repetition of these strokes from, say, a few rounds of five to ten, up to several rounds at the speed of one hundred and twenty breaths per minute months later. To enjoy maximum benefit from this preparation, contract the sphincter muscles throughout the exercise. It is not unusual to feel heightened vigor and mental clarity following this practice, but dizziness may occur if one stands erect right after the practice.

- Sit comfortably erect with both feet on the floor.

- Begin breathing diaphragmatically, then vigorously and quickly push your abdominal muscles inward as you exhale the air through your nose. The quick expulsion makes a rushing sound through the nostrils, as though you were blowing your nose. Do not hold the contraction inward but release it naturally. The movement resembles a snapping motion with the force on the exhalation.

- Immediately allow the abdomen to expand without force by inhaling naturally.
- Repeat this procedure five times in quick succession; then breathe normally for five breaths.

This breathing practice puts stimulating pressure upon your inner organs. Allow a few weeks of practice in order to condition your lungs and increase endurance. Practice daily and every few days increase the number of breaths in each sequence. You should get to the point where you can perform the exercise for five minutes without feeling any strain. Whenever you begin to feel depleted in energy from the rush of the day, rejuvenate your energy with this breathing exercise. The more you use it, the easier it becomes.

As you become familiar with these breathing practices, there is a gradual cleansing of the body from noxious gases and a toning of the respiratory muscles. Combined with this improvement, a subtler psychological effect ensues. Introducing these breathing exercises primes the body and mind for meditation. But remember that their benefits require first-hand experience for confirmation.

Breath Bonus

America loves being active. We have 85 million cyclists, 72 million hikers, 50 million fishermen, 30 million runners, and 25 million golfers. They seem to shout, "Who wants to sit in the dark?" We think these active individuals would give up meditation as bothersome or not to their taste. Let's try a different tack.

Leave aside the inward art and become a born-again breather. Byron Nelson, professional golfer, offhandedly remarked on his unprecedented string of winnings that the key for him resided in the regulation of his breath. Slip the deliberate act of breathing into the activity of choice. Occasionally return to a self-conscious sense of regulated respiration and note the difference it makes in how you feel. Feel stressed at times? Don't force your mind's ideas to deal with your constrictions; instead, try trusting your breathing.

Now just shut your mouth, and let diaphragmatic motion become your norm.

Charting
the
Elusive
Mind

To appreciate the art of meditation by understanding its inherent dynamism requires various descriptions to explicate the vast topic. These next chapters thus give the new practitioner a sense of finding his way about the inner territory, including the repercussions of the mind's pervasion of the human body. Whatever repetition occurs will be cast to bring out further explanations.

Applying for a new job demands submission of your resume. This information yields a portrait of your work history and skills. No one would insist that this designation totally summarizes your creative potential, but it indisputably shows how you have pursued reality and thus understood yourself in career ways. While meditation may not enhance these business skills, it will definitely show you the origin of the creative source of those skills. In fact, the action of learning about that source becomes itself a skillful endeavor that demands recurring actions on the part of the seeker.

To understand the enormous resourcefulness of

meditation it is necessity to consider this principle: who and what I make of myself is first and foremost a product of my mind. It is so easy to forget, overlook, or deny this elementary truth. How one regards oneself flows directly into every action that one does, personal or business. Meditation is no exception.

To say it in other words, I contribute to my environment, my family, my business, my health, my hopes themselves, by informing my mind. First I configure my mind – an idea, a plan, a series of concepts – and then I implement that form into the environment. Whatever I hope to produce in the environment has already occurred in my mind. I also retain an archive of those productive efforts in my memory as well as in my subconscious mind.

The mind can likewise reform the environment. From having you cut overgrown hedges that you planted to renovating your garage, the mind can modify what it has formed. Whatever happens occurs first in the mind and last in the real world. Human actions are more than tangible extensions of the idea; they have an impact on the performer. Hence the formation of habits.

In meditation, however, a different tack is taken. Here your mind neither forms nor reforms. Instead, you reside with the power that forms or reforms. The act of meditation is not attending to the formation of a new idea, no matter how sublime. It is a choiceful act, allowing your attention to become uninvolved and very still. One does not direct the mind to compose, ponder, or implement ideas. Instead, one directs attention to be at rest. It is a refusal to form new ideas or play with the imagination. In meditation, you, the knower, suspend the act of knowing from conceiving new ideas or rehashing old ones.

At first it's not that easy. Some of the notions that occupy the memory region of the mind, the unconscious level, have a simmering insistence. Like prima donnas, they want attention. After all, you have resorted to them time and time again. Some taunt you, like the Sirens lured Odysseus; their configurations are irresistible. These familiar ideas have become so very much a part of your personality, distressful or not, that without them you would be hampered, perhaps desperate, to sustain the continuity from yesterday's being who you were to today's being the same person. Imagine what daily life would be like without a reliable memory. We are creatures of memory more than we realize.

In meditation we turn our attention inward and come face to face with those current ideas and phantoms from the past that are dear to our personal survival, even if they are painful. This inner confrontation is not meant to be dramatic or seen as a punishment, although it certainly can assume those proportions. There are occasionally some intensely emotional disclosures that demand attention, but the mind simply views these emerging ideas that it has already formed and invested with some degree of emotional self-interest. In facing them, there is no need for self-incrimination. Neither is it an occasion for outrage. Humor, perhaps, but more likely boredom eventuates. Now what?

The Crucial Response

Regulating your breath and withdrawing your senses from contact with the environment has caught your rational mind off guard. With no new sense impressions to organize, the rational mind accedes to its partner, the unconscious, with its own surging contents. There you are, gazing upon the fluctuating contents of your train of thoughts, each vying for your undivided attention. Forget about trying to halt the parade. What is important is to not get involved again, emotionally or intellectually, regardless of the fascination of these ideas.

Now you must become shrewd. You need to perform the simple act of uninvolved recognition: just witness the mind's streaming contents. Hands off. Period. Poised, allow the flow of ideas uninterrupted passage through your mind. This marks the profound inauguration of the meditator's transformation. Consequently, previously expressed, as well as unexpressed, information begins to emerge, sometimes even repetitively, upon the mind's screen. The trick is to stay uninvolved, poised, unattached.

Meditation is not diligently sifting through the stuff of the unconsciousness. To call upon your analytic ability to decipher these scenes detours you from the meditative process. If meditation were simply the counting of ideas, feelings, and images that emerge before the mind, then meditation would be an endless task no different from an audit of your taxes. Enumeration and assessment are important mental functions, but you will want to retire them during your inward journey.

The meditative process is the steady, persistent avoidance of the active use of the mind's discursive faculty by keeping steady awareness. Most of our waking hours engage this discursive faculty, which makes it difficult to turn our attention away from it. We don't tell it to "turn off," for then we would assume a defensive state of mind in which our attention, instead of pursuing silence, would spend its energy halting the irrepressive, discursive process.

The spontaneous emergence of thoughts and feelings surfaces naturally before human attention. It can't be helped. These uninvited, but intrusive, occurrences evoke exasperation. "Why don't they stop emerging?" we ask, or more importantly, "Why don't they go away?" Of course we assume that progress is out of the question since they recur so incessantly. It seems very disheartening to encounter these changing contents day after day.

Progress in meditation is not an aggressive attempt to obliterate these thoughts from our consciousness. It is a matter of purposefully becoming *indifferent* to their fleeting presence. At the beginning one needs a reminder to not expend efforts in avoiding their emergence and to instead direct attention in a steady focus upon the object of meditation. Holding a steady focus of attention, rather than repressing thought forms, is the goal of your endeavor.

When Caesar Millan, The Dog Whisperer on television, encounters pet problems in the homes of dog owners who invite his counsel, more often than not the issue is the failure of the owners to assume intelligent control over their pet. The owners are so sincere in their fondness for the animal that they cannot seem to understand why the dog won't behave properly.

The point is not any deficiency in love but in understanding and respecting the nature of the human-animal relationship. Millan notes that unless one asserts intelligent dominance, which the pet expects, then the animal fills in the negligence and predictably runs the show.

Likewise, unless the meditator assumes command over his imagination and thought processes, then those powers, like the pet, will arbitrarily run his life as well as his practice. We need to assertively remind ourselves every now and then exactly what we want our minds to do. The act of witnessing is a firm choice.

Swami Rama stated that at times one needs to rally the mind to refuse the internal distractions that plague our meditation practice. Literally, one can block the continuation of distracting images by exclaiming "No!" interiorly. Unsolicited images and ideas will remain the bane of meditation unless we exert our power to call the shots.

The Practical Rule

There is an idea, a practical rule that seems to manifest after some experience in the practice of meditation. It is: don't fight with the mind; just stay aloof. The sudden appearance of unexpected ideas and feelings in the mind is not a failure in meditation. There are no penalties, nor should there be guilt accruing for undiscriminating thoughts as they surface into our awareness. Meditation is not the calm expectation of another stream of thoughts in order to become disinterested with them. The inexorable flow of ideas and future plans, once you close your eyes, is a retained byproduct of your involvement in experiencing the world.

Eventually, sitting to meditate and allowing the breath rhythm to establish itself permits the mind to return to a more unexpressed state. By becoming less interested in forming new concepts or rehashing old ones, you will feel, faintly at first, a sense of renewal and inner composure.

This renewal is like sending the mind on a holiday. A genuine vacation always restores. Getting your mind off pressures and demands, just like taking a holiday, eventually leaves behind the worries of the ordinary day and allows you to proceed further into and past your mind.

Being at ease with the mind produces another surprise.

You begin to sense more control over the ordinary tendencies of the imagination to form ideas and react to them. It is now easier to make yourself emotionally enthralled. Ever so gradually, you sense that your emotional responses are much more under your control than you can previously remember them being.

People assign to meditation various purposes. From the reduction of stressful feelings to stimulating creativity, compelling reasons can be selected. The finality of meditation, however, if you let it run its natural course, is not arbitrary. It's nothing less than total self-disclosure with self-control of all the hidden aspects, dimensions, levels, and realms of your consciousness. In meditation, you leave all sorrows behind to understand the understander.

The
Unconscious
Realm

Modern education teaches us about ideas and the various sensory ways we can arrive at understanding the world at large. We may take a course in biology, for example, with textbooks, laboratory exposure, and perhaps field trips to discover first-hand the vast realm of nature and its workings in a careful and observant manner. The fascinating field trips afford a personal affair with nature far beyond just reading ideas about it in a botany book. Now the budding biologist has raw experience to ponder and can judge the textbook's contents through experience. The responsibility of the course ends there with the student. Equipped with the tools of the trade, the student is able to move on into further studies.

The Functions of Consciousness

After sufficient time in the practice of meditation, one can also reflect upon one's personal exposure to the art and discover another vast territory: the hidden or unconscious realm of the mind and its many workings. Our rational or discursive mind normally used in every science, art, craft, business enterprise, or personal decision, is now, thanks to exposure to meditation, available for understanding its inherent nature. Unique in this investigation is the fact that the act of meditation joins the person who actually is the laboratory, the investigator, and also the field trip. In the physical sciences, the object of study is an independent subject matter outside the student. In meditation, however, the object of study is the subject matter inside oneself: the mind in its various acts of performance.

The discursive mind can apply its own act of knowing to itself in its mindful activity. In other words, the mind knows itself in its very act of being a reasoning mind. This incredible association is possible since the mind's power literally instigates its own activity of pondering, willing, or imaging as well as its own mental products, which are concepts, ideas, and even the execution of its bodily behavior. The mind naturally becomes enthralled with its own operation. Since it can know what it's doing throughout its mental processes all along the way, it can also monitor itself while performing its own activity. One can watch oneself in action and then intervene in the process.

Since we can retain these various episodes of our mind in action, the unconscious realm becomes the museum of all sorts of symbolic paraphernalia. The contents of our unconscious mind are so subtle at times that we cannot anticipate their emergence. We often mistake certain feelings and thoughts for reality, while they are actually our own temporary mood or a flare-up of a previous emotion. Then, of course, there are occasions in daily life, like the people we meet, unexpected events, episodes in our personal careers, that awaken past memories tucked away in our minds.

Our memory works through a process of association, and the environment easily stimulates it. Memories bubble up to the surface from our history. Past experiences sometimes tumble into the path of our current concentration and attract our attention. "Why did I feel this way when I met that person? Why did I react so strongly? It seemed out of proportion to the event that was happening."

We see or hear something, and suddenly we remember a past episode. "Now why did I associate this current experience with that particular memory?" Sometimes the association is obvious, and the mind stays preoccupied with it, chattering in spite of our preference. At times, we feel hopelessly incapable of altering our attention from these uncomfortable, incessant ideas and feelings. The wake-up call is about to come.

The reason the call has not been heard yet is that we have not gone through a new stage of self-discovery just waiting to occur. Instead, we eagerly fulfill the recurring adage: "I use my mind so much in the same way that I can't but help get the same fitful results." We're so busy endorsing the same ideas and indulging their accompanying emotions, that we do not realize that at the same time we expect to evade the same weary consequences. We forget that the task of finding out the meaning of life may involve, but does not belong to, the body, emotions, rational ideas, career, genes, politics, or marital prospects.

Meditation, in regard to the activities of the unconscious, takes on the job of expanding our awareness into that hidden realm to such an extent that our habitual mental preoccupations with unnecessary matters gradually appear less important to us, perhaps even petty. We begin to see things for what they are. Due to this broadening of awareness, it dawns on us that maybe we ourselves are the primary cause of the way we think and feel, rather than the situation itself or a remark made by someone else. This is not a one-night fling to self-discovery, however. We do not instantly emerge a master surveyor of all the hidden regions of consciousness. Even the Buddha had a run for his money!

Let's ponder the implications of a situation if the very wellspring of our creativity – vital energy, healing power, the ability to communicate – would be in our daily self-awareness, at our beck and call rather than, as is so often the case, only asserting itself episodically. We know how frustrating and disappointing that can be. Often we want to do something, but we just can't seem to get in the mood; or the mood won't last, and we've got a deadline.

Most of our mind is not under our direct control in an easy and efficient way, and that is why life is neither as steady nor as spontaneously cheerful as we would like it to be. Every now and then a "demon" pops up, and we're thrown by the images and ideas provoked by that occurrence. By steadily working with the practice of meditation, however, we create an inner atmosphere whereby our depth of awareness begins to expand beyond its self-imposed boundaries shaped by clinging to our problems and finally exposes these "demons" for the fiction that they are.

Many of us have always suspected that there are further levels of knowledge within. We know that we are not just a sense being, emotionally reacting to life. We know there are exceedingly strong subtleties within us that can't be reduced to sensation. The fact that we can use words like "friendship," "love," and "justice" indicates that there are experiences that cannot be resolved back to the sense level.

Animals normally don't ponder these verities, but you and I do because we know that we are more than our bodies, more than just a reflection of the pleasant or unpleasant moods at our sense levels. True, we like the excitement that's engendered by being in contact with the tangible, but after a while it begins to pale. Most of us could not spend all day pursuing only sensations; it's not enriching enough. Our nature provides us with certain signals that clamor, "Come on, let's go further, deeper, wider. Let's find levels beyond this body that we need to grasp in order to be satisfied, in order to understand life."

Neither drugs nor repression are the remedy for these signals, as both compound the issue. It is incredibly silly to pose that imbibing a chemical can get one into spiritual territory. Evading the challenge forestalls the day of reckoning, at best. The practice of meditation aids us by slowly widening our ability to integrate all the aspects of our personalities while understanding their limitations. Then we can live out the truth that's already in us at that level. When we understand what constitutes sensations and emotions and how they affect our mind, then we're much freer to engage the situations that provoke those levels of response. The breakthrough hits when we realize that some indispensable questions and personal issues cannot be remedied at the body level or the rational level; they are too important for those levels of truth.

Meditation Reveals the Intelligence of Spirit

A human person is a multi-leveled being. Our nature not only shares sensations with the animal level, but we also share our being with the vegetable and mineral kingdoms. In other words, we already comprise all the levels that constitute the realm of nature. We are a microcosm within the macrocosm. All the principles and elements that are in nature and the universe are contained within us.

But being human implies something unique because, in addition to all those elements, we have a unique power, one which sets us light-years beyond the empirical universe.

We can be aware of all those elements that comprise our being and be conscious of ourself. We have the remarkable ability to apprehend the material life around us in a non-material way so that we literally become one with it by understanding it. True understanding is a spiritual unity between the knower and the knowable world.

A caution is needed here, however. In learning about life, by using the mind to expand our comprehension of nature and the cosmos, we can unify with something and yet be trapped by that knowledge. We can choose to make it more important than it is in itself. We can set up a new "demon."

When we use the power of our mind to fabricate something that's really not there, we presume that the end product is authentic. When it's not appreciated by others, or if it disappoints us, pain and sadness result, along with frustration and anger. Frequently this happens when we invest more value in the object, the person, the event, or the activity than is really warranted. Our expectations rise, but the future does not unfold as we expected. We feel that life let us down because it did not measure up to our expectations. This juncture is where meditation sounds the wake-up call.

Our mind pursues life because it can't help it; its very nature has a proclivity to embrace the totality of the universe. The human soul is a miniature cosmos, and our destiny is to bring that totality into a contemplative vision. "You are a nucleus, and your expansion is the universe," my teacher loved to repeat. To know the absolute is to become absolutely free!

We have a nature that relishes cognitive and affective experiences, since our inner dynamism thrusts us toward reality. We are born into a flight toward that vast understanding. From pursuing new hobbies to visiting lands that pique our curiosity, to the uniqueness of a new grandchild and the excitement of discovery, we want to embrace all that life offers. It becomes self-evident that the inner dynamism toward the experience of life constitutes a natural law of our being. We must comprehend the ultimate meaning of existence.

Some truths of life will not endure; they're not meant to last. These truths reside at a relative level of understanding. We bake a cake, go jogging, change jobs, or move to new residences. True acts, but how long do they last? How long is the food you ate for lunch going to remain as food? Through the day we experience reality in different ways, on different terms of existence. Some things remain with us longer than others; some things, by their very nature, are only temporary. All can affect us in some way. When something touches our intelligence, there is perhaps, no discernible change; we don't weigh more or grow taller. We seem to look the same as we did before, but we may be learning magnificent truths about life. The experience enlarges our self-understanding.

It's a strange paradox. If we assimilate something material, our personal quantity increases, and yet we can only accept so much. After a meal, for example, we may say, "That's enough; I'm done. I'll have more tomorrow, but today I'm filled." Bodily matter is very definitely limited. Such sensation, while beneficial, is short-lived. But do you ever say, "No, I don't want you to love me any more; I don't want our friendship to deepen" or "I don't want to know more about truth; I know enough about the mystery of life"? We rarely reject love or truth. Rather, we feel compelled to have and know more.

The human spirit is of another order of reality. We can't stop wanting more; and the more we obtain, the more we want. Knowing and loving what we know are at the heart of our being. The thirst of the spirit is un-quenchable because, as the ancients mention, we are made for the infinite.

Unlike matter, spirit cannot suffer entropy. No corrosion, nothing stale, always fresh, warranted for eternity. This does not mean that the body is bad; it means that the body is limited, subject to time and space. The body isn't evil; it's just that its truth is limited. We can only do so much with the matter of the body by itself. In spite of its marvelous agility and dexterity, its natural truth is quite relative; it can't reach out in knowledge and love toward reality.

Yet if I ignore the basic, common-sense laws of taking care of my living body, thinking that somehow my spiritual endeavors are superior to its needs, or that I'm somehow holier for my asceticism, more advanced because

I disregard my health, that again is a demon, leading to pain and sorrow.

The key to human fulfillment, human realization, is integration. If we want to reach the realms of consciousness, we don't ignore the body. Instead, we find out how the body and the spirit relate, and we learn what the laws are that guard and preserve that marvelous relationship. We don't just jump out of the body when we decide to become spiritual.

When we examine their personal lives, we learn that genuine sages never endorsed abuse of the body. In one ancient tradition, in fact, the body is clearly understood to be a temple, something sacred. Why? Because within it dwells the supreme spirit of infinite intelligence. The spirit animates the body, and thus a living, desired inter-relationship resides between the two.

What makes a human body more than matter is the presence of the spirit; what makes the spirit humanly present is its embodiment in matter. What makes matter alive, and not like stone, is the fact that a vibrant life force pervades it. In a way, to neglect the body is to neglect the spirit as it exists in the body. Our spirit is giving life to our mind as well as to every cell in our body. Therefore, we have to understand and acknowledge the operational laws at each level of our being. If we don't, then it's not possible to integrate that level of our person in a coordinated, intelligent, peaceful way. There is a price to be paid for this omission. What ought to be cared for becomes suppressed, and our suppressions and misconceptions inhabit the subconscious and become the brooding "devils" that interfere with discovering the truth of life. Again, it is meditation that sounds our wake-up call.

The Infrastructure of Awareness

We are a complex unity. The body-mind unity is so intimately related that thought and feeling, intellect and emotion, affectation and cognition, mutually affect one another. If I think a certain way, gland secretion prepares my body to assist the corporeal direction of my thought. An obvious example is the act of dwelling on a remembered episode of anger or sadness. One's whole body is affected via the nervous system. The entire person feels the mood. In the magnificent psychosomatic relationship there is not a thought we can think that will not provoke an emotion. Under the influence of ideas, the body changes; under the influence of emotion, the mind changes. To find the real amid the changes of life, to find stability amid the flux of matter, to find security of mind amid the misfortunes of personal history, a different kind of experience is required. We mean an experience of spirit alone, without the active body and discursive reasoning being directly involved. We mean a reality within that unifies and pacifies all levels of our embodied being.

Neither emotions nor discursive reasoning reaches that reality, for it is meditation's home field. In meditation

we meet the inner obstacles, those self-limiting ideas
that prevent us from knowing our own nature as it truly
exists. With patience, a new release of pacifying calmness
emerges, enabling an integration of body and mind rooted
in the harmonious rhythms of breathing. Subconscious
memories then surface before the mind's eye. The
emotionally-tinged thoughts gradually subside because
the dynamism of meditation reconstitutes the body-mind
complex into its natural state of balanced repose.

From the vantage point of tranquility, we can measure
our investment in life more accurately as we sustain in
our daily activities the steady clarity of mind derived
from meditation. Former tendencies to disturbance will
gradually yield. A growing sense of tranquil integration is
recognized and preserved longer during the day. Although
we slip, we know how to recover its presence and prefer
more and more to judge life from its perspective. Instead
of regarding our subconscious as a haunted house, we can
draw upon its power for creative insight into the world
at large. Through this creative awareness we will slowly
become aware of the magnitude of our nature and the
fulfillment of our destiny.

Swami Rama tells the following story, which happens
to be one of my favorites:

One evening, after my brother disciple and I had
walked thirty miles in the mountains, we stopped
to rest two miles past Badrinath. I was very tired
and soon fell asleep, but my sleep was restless

because of my extreme fatigue. It was cold and I didn't have a blanket to wrap around me, so I put my hands around my neck to keep warm. I rarely dream. I've dreamt only three or four times in my life, and all of my dreams came true. That night I dreamed that the devil was choking my throat with strong hands, and I felt as though I were suffocating. When my brother disciple saw my breath rhythm change and realized that I was experiencing considerable discomfort, he came to me and woke me up. I said, "Somebody was choking my throat." He told me that my own hands were choking my throat! That which you call the devil is part of you, and the myth of the devil and of evil is imposed on us by our own ignorance. The human mind is a great wonder and magician; it can assume the form of both the devil or hero any time it wishes. It can be a fearsome enemy or a inspiring friend, creating either hell or heaven for us. We choose our own destiny.

Becoming
a Witness

In trying to keep your attention at one point – the space between your eyebrows, for instance – you will notice very soon that your mind resists sustaining this inward focus. That resistance shows up with a whole gamut of "stuff" running through your head: images, feelings, ideas, sounds, flickering lights, feelings of body tensions, itching, muscular releases, and so on.

You have launched into the inner darkness, expecting profound serenity and high states of knowledge. You expected to make the Meditation Olympic Team within a few weeks, entertaining out-of-body experiences, reading people's minds, indisputably knowing the future. Instead, every kind of distraction taunts your sincere efforts to remain steadily focused. Even rational declarations occur to you: "Why am I doing this? It seems a waste of time, when there are so many tasks to fulfill. Maybe it just isn't for me. I could be doing other things that require my attention. Perhaps when I get older." The litany continues and you finally arrive at the inexorable conclusion that you aren't getting it. How are you going to make the Olympic Team if this problem keeps afflicting your sincere efforts?

Obviously, you neither beckoned forth these negative thoughts nor had any idea of what to expect. In spite of your best efforts to remain thoughtless, you seemed doomed to failure. You may have even shut off any new outside information through your senses. Nevertheless, your mind continues to conjure ideas, images, reminiscences. At times, you feel badgered. Is it not curious that you can't stay away from the ramblings of the mind?

Here's the secret to dealing with this problem: don't try to fight with your mind; don't try to stop your thoughts! Your job in meditation is just to note what's going on and do nothing about it. Keep no engagement with ideas or images. Instead, you are to maintain the stance of being aloof. You are a casual bystander. You are a mental tourist, noting the train of activity fluctuating before your mind's eye. Remaining a witness is your sole occupation.

Should you get caught off guard and drift into one of the thoughts or items, you'll suddenly find yourself entertaining a thought process. Don't waste time condemning yourself or getting upset; just drop the idea and continue to notice. And don't be surprised how often this slipping may return. Fond and not-so-fond memories will appear before you. Events you haven't pondered in years will reassert themselves. Guilt, joy, fear, worry? It doesn't matter. Remember, you are merely a witness. Progress in meditation requires that aspirants assertively confront these uninvited guests.

Mantras

For serious seekers, the Himalayan Tradition, and a few others, offers sound vibrations, *mantras,* for accelerating progress. The utterance of a mantra is not arbitrary, however. Contrary to our democratic culture, the selection of a sacred sound is not an individual choice, nor are prayers a substitute for mantras. Many sincere Americans are deluded into thinking that mantras are fashionable accoutrements. Some entrepreneurial teachers advertise all sorts of mantra inducements, claiming to elicit enlightenment for you. *Caveat emptor* cannot be emphasized enough. As Swami Rama of the Himalayas tells us:

> A mantra is a combination of syllables or words corresponding to a particular energy vibration. The student, when initiated by a qualified teacher, utilizes the mantra received as his object for meditation, and as he practices over a period of time, it gradually leads his meditation deeper and deeper. It is the condensed essence of all the teaching the *guru* has to give a student, and it is only through his constant practice of *japa* (repetition of the mantra) within meditation and in his active life that the power of the mantra and its essential teaching will gradually unfold as its latent mental and spiritual energies are released.

Although lists of various mantras can be found in texts, their actual dispersal and implementation requires a representative teacher. Repeating mantras with fervor is powerless unless the initiation has taken place. When a student is initiated into a tradition, these unique sounds are dispensed by the tradition, not invented by the initiator, who is only the messenger. Without that authoritative connection, the repetition of a mantra is impotent; when, however the bond is set, the full power of the tradition stands with the student.

A Breakthrough

One day it will hit you: ideas are just temporary inhabitants. In other words, you have kept your ideas sequestered in your memory bank, that portion of the mind known as the unconscious. Looking back, you obviously have entertained countless ideas and feelings over a lifetime. Important agendas, exciting plans, high hopes, even disappointments, color your life as well as everyone else's. You must have also noticed that ideas have careers. However necessary and important, one day a treasured notion will have run its unexpected course. You retire it to the nostalgic dustbin of the past. While you probably hold certain ideas dear and almost priceless, you have changed your mind about many items innumerable times.

Just ponder: you are the thinker, not the thought; the feeler, not the felt emotion; the experiencer, not the experience. You remember but you are not the things remembered. You are so much more than your ideas or feelings. Your identity is neither defined nor confined by any company resume. The freedom that you have from this insight is intriguing. Gradually, with practice, you will release any and all impediments and self-imposed restrictions that you harbor within yourself, including unreasonable fears, angers, guilt, grievances, and so forth, before the intense power of witnessing.

Reinventing Yourself

Gaze within. One motivation of meditation practice is to observe the contents of your mind rather than to deny their alternating presence. This difference is important. The active, rational mind will run its course. Attempting to prevent the flux of ideas is futile; suppression has no business in meditation. Your job is simply to hold your gaze. The mind's stance in this practice has no other purpose than witnessing. How long a thought lingers does not matter. What kind of idea appears does not matter. You are the onlooker. Just notice.

We seem to forget that ideas, however grandiose and rewarding, are temporary configurations with no permanent standing by themselves. Mental forms come and go, appear and disappear. Through witnessing them you come to recognize their impermanent status. This recognition cannot be forced. After some time, the profound impact of not being essentially associated with your ideas of yourself occurs spontaneously.

Sometimes there is fear associated with the recognition of the impermanence of thought forms, the *vrittis* as they are known in the ancient language of Sanskrit. Ideas get to be like old friends as well as familiar enemies. You prefer to have the mind occupied by them. Even your unfriendly thoughts, like an undesirable tenant, stick around.

Keeping the mind too preoccupied on ideas of how you currently see yourself and what life is about restricts your self-understanding. There are moments when a newer insight appears, but often this is dismissed or censored by the prevailing notion, large or small, of your self-importance. Gradually, you will see that you are more than the continual flow of ideas that rule your attention.

Witnessing is Unique

Ideas, like images, are accidental changes. The act of witnessing, however, is not an accidental change from one moment to the next. The act of witnessing stems from your substantial nature, for it can perdure amid and throughout vast conceptual and emotional changes. It need not lose its stance when concepts and images are replaced by subsequent ones.

The act of witnessing is not in conflict with personal endeavors. Being personally concerned about life is not imperiled by the practice of paying attention. Most people rework their thoughts more than need be. Preoccupation tires. Instead of being fresh and calm, they dissipate their energy into being emotionally concerned with petty and trivial thoughts.

If you think about pleasant or unpleasant thoughts, you will soon experience the feelings associated with them. If you rehearse emotional dramas, then you are taking an active role in them, even though each drama originates in your mind. The more you deliberately reassociate, the more things stay the same.

When you *witness* the melodrama, on the other hand, then you will experience something different from the feeling associated with its contents. Rather than re-participate in the role, you now experience something else that lets you be untouched by the appearance of the drama. This measure of objectivity needs to be confirmed again and again. The mind is like the open sky, entertaining all kinds of weather. In the sky of meditation allow your thoughts, like wind-blown clouds, to just pass by.

Wrestling with My Mind

For beginners meditation is a struggle. The struggle takes place upon the mind's terrain. My concepts, feelings, and images belong, as far as I am concerned, to me. No doubt some of my ideas are beneficial. My employment and my social identity depend upon them. In that sense I am responsible for them.

While being entertained by our ideas and profiting from them, a larger sense of our identity is always there in the background. In our excitement with the task at hand we forget the larger picture, not perceiving a differentiation between "my" ideas and the "me" who thinks them and executes them.

In the act of witnessing, a certain personal loosening from our ideas occurs. The fact that we notice them without analyzing or articulating them or allowing ourselves to get excited about them means that one has more freedom over the mind than we might have presumed. "I the thinker" generate and communicate ideas and images, change my mind about them, even feel their impact in my emotions, but I have yet to seriously understand that they are not irreplaceable.

At first this experience seems strange, not only because it is new but especially because it feels so intangible. I have always associated my mind with activity. Now I aspire for a non-participative silence. Now I widen my awareness beyond the cognitive activity of ideas and schemes into what feels like a no man's land of emptiness. A new sense of inner space looms. Like an astronaut soaring beyond the recognition of the planetary bodies into the darkness of the unknown, I sit there quietly in my simple gaze. Meditation welcomes me to the dark void.

This sense of emptiness is quite normal, but it is not insubstantial. It is a reality more real than the thoughts, feelings, or images that you will ever entertain. For a long while you will feel uneasy, repeatedly feeling skeptical about what exactly is going on. These doubts about your so-called progress are almost periodic but not catastrophic. In this no man's land there are no overwhelming sound bites to indicate that everything is coming along quite fine. Actually there are definite clues, but in your present state of ambiguity you doubt them, too. Later as familiarity with meditation sets in, they will become self-evident.

Meditation's First Level of Mind

When sitting with your eyes closed, your attention enters the first corridor of the mind. This corridor is the busiest level. Thoughts, images, and feelings emerge and then vanish. By bringing your attention inward, away from bodily senses, a new appreciation for the busyness of the mind comes to light. It seems like an inner attack by thoughts, with one thought tumbling after another to capture attention. The mind's activity at this level is like watching a television set whose channels constantly change every few seconds. This relentless situation is not extraordinary; it is quite normal.

The process of meditation does not mean shutting down thoughts. The rational mind has a normal bias; it seeks sense impressions and generates thoughts. Hence it resists quieting itself. The key to meditation is not to oppose this rational level but to expand attention to a different level of consciousness.

People expect and obtain a variety of experiences from meditation: everything from striking images to bright lights, from unusual sounds to sudden ideas. And certain phenomena may occur periodically. One may lose bodily awareness. One's serenity may reach a depth where sensual perception of one's anatomy virtually vanishes. No physical harm results, but we identify so intensely with our bodies that this profoundly peaceful interlude may shock us. Some may note that a pulsation occurs between the eyebrows. Again, this is a natural sign, indicating that the body-mind complex is being integrated for an expansion of awareness. Gradually, these events will become habitual, and you will not notice them so much. They are among the many milestones along the way for your benefit.

Those things may persist for awhile, but then a shift occurs. There will be less variety and more sameness. Boredom will easily set in. Reaching this stage, students inevitably complain: "Nothing ever happens!" Correct. But for the student, skepticism mounts. The reason for doubt is that the mind is getting used to existing in a state of simple awareness rather than always resorting to thought forms and sound. A new stage is entered. If you will endure the boredom, a sense of inner consolidation will occur: the taste of silence.

Meditation will help you discover the revelation of silence. That is a new way of understanding the aware-ness of your being. You will truly be in another space level in your mind, one that does not depend for its existence upon cogitating ideas. The very fact that you are aware of thought forms passing before your mind proves that a widening has occurred.

In other words, your act of awareness is not focused upon images and ideas. Sitting quietly enlarges your awareness beyond the normal contents of your rational mind, no matter how important. Whether there are thought forms or not, your inner stance now is one of steadying your attention by simply being aware. It almost seems un-American to just sit there without engaging the mind in thinking about something, but it is correct.

Much later meditation will affect mythic perceptions. One will find all of life impressive and awesomely beautiful. Intrigued by the simplest of things, the mind will become a clear mirror, able to reflect the world as it in itself.

The
Inner
Science

With the method of meditation in hand, you are now able to begin the journey. In our times we have associated the notion of validity with empirical evidence. If it's real, it's touchable. If it's true, it's tangible.

The question then logically arises about whether our inner journey can measure up to the canons of science. Meditation invites us to investigate, not our brain, but a more intangible reality that isn't so easily discernable. The claim of meditation, while not obviously empirically evident from the perspective of conventional science, nevertheless asserts itself as a scientific endeavor.

Modern science is indisputably predicated upon its ability to verify its hypotheses. Verification is quite important because it allows the investigator to confirm his thoughts objectively and thus make them publicly scrutable. In astronomy, for example, scientists may not be sensibly aware that there is another planet in their field of current examination, yet they hypothesize the existence of an undisclosed planet based on the data of the perturbations of other heavenly bodies. Through their ingenuity, scientific investigators can occasionally predict the discovery of a new heavenly body. Some of the planets in our solar system, Neptune, for example, have been located this way.

An elementary textbook in physics may assert that plain water (H_2O) boils at 212 degrees Fahrenheit. But how does anyone really know that that statement is true? How do I know it makes sense? Is the author conjecturing? Does water really boil at this point? The author may be a close friend, or he may even possess a Nobel Prize in Science, but are those assurances sufficient to make me feel secure in the knowledge that water boils at 212 degrees? Hardly; without experiencing the fact, without proving it to myself, doubts arise.

I want to experience the reality of boiling water at that degree. My mind isn't satisfied with anything less. In other words, a scientific demonstration requires first-hand knowledge. Second-hand knowledge, textbook statements, and words from an authority cannot guarantee the veracity of knowledge.

Whether we are professionals striving to examine or comprehend a section of reality, or just lay people who are interested in life in general, we prefer real facts to wishful hoping. To stay close to the facts of life helps us to deal intelligently with the task of life. With facts, we have more possibilities for success in living than just hoping or praying that things will work out.

Today, meditation is being recognized in research circles as a scientific fact with humanistic value. Interestingly, the procedures and methodology for exploring meditation are unique. Meditation's subject matter is distinguished by the investigator's being his own laboratory. The investigator, in the practice of meditation, experiments with experience – his own inner experience.

Broadly speaking, there are two regions available to scientific endeavor: those that deal with outer phenomena – the sensible, obvious world and its subtle implication – and those that deal with the interior phenomenon of consciousness. This latter region is where the science of meditation stakes its claim.

In its search for secure knowledge, science attempts to establish its hypotheses by eliminating the variables and finding the constant factors in the experiment. Likewise, meditation follows the same procedure. As a science, meditation hypothesizes that the investigator can discover, in an orderly and repeatable fashion, universal knowledge regarding the conscious nature of human beings. Moreover, the methodological procedures carried on in the experiment are capable of verification by disinterested investigators. By submitting to the objectivity of verification, meditation removes itself from the onus of anecdotal experience.

Before outlining the meditation experiment in broad strokes, let us begin with some preliminary fact-finding at the common sense level of ordinary introspection and reflection on human experiences. Introspection will be used as a procedural tool throughout the experiment, but the investigator will refine it as he probes further into the experiment. In a normal day, the experimenter notices that the mind and body entertain all kinds of changes. From the endless succession of concepts and images to the equally unending bodily sensations, moods, temperature, and anatomical modifications, the experimenter-meditator undergoes almost relentless alteration. The meditator as subject matter seemingly resembles a constantly fluctuating variable. At this preliminary stage, neither the mind nor the body would qualify as constants in the experiment, for both are patently variables. The question, therefore, is whether the body-mind complex in its variable status exhausts the evidence that composes the nature of the meditator.

Granted that the body and the mind fluctuate throughout the day, each of us still feels that we are always, in some way, the same individual who undergoes these changes. For example, I am thinking about the weather; I am feeling the cool rain; I am stretching; I am resenting your intrusion; I am getting hungry; I am missing my friends; I cannot recall what I wanted to remember – these and untold more episodes occur to the same person all in one day. As yesterday, so tomorrow. Throughout the changes in body and mind, the same "I" persists as the experiencer.

Whether one experiences the life of the mind as a series of fluid configurations or a stack of contiguous snapshots, something abides in spite of the unpredictable and illogical occurrences of ideas that blur into each other. Something renders continuity to these many occurrences. Life is hardly a quilt of isolated experiences seamed together by the incidental threads of time, space, and location. While waking, dreaming, and sleeping may comprise my apparent range of experiences, in between these traveled states I do not suffer annihilation. Something about me sustains its existence without changing amid the changes experienced. Without some perdurable, underlying reality upon which these mental and bodily changes take place, human change would put itself out of business. Human changes cannot exist in and by themselves; they occur or take place in an existing human reality. The experiencer has a sense of self-awareness as he undergoes all the changes.

Given this brief review of human experience simply to introduce the experiment, one now tests the original hypothesis by carefully setting up the conditions recommended in a traditional manner. First, a stationary sitting posture is assumed, eyes are closed, and rhythmic is breathing is commenced − all for the purpose of subduing the fluctuating variables. A systematic process is undergone by the experimenter, who attentively directs, controls, and observes the self-induced experiment. The relaxed stationary posture settles the body while the rhythmic breathing settles the nervous system and calms the imagination. The experimenter gradually focuses his inner attention in a designated manner that permits him to witness the entire quieting process. As the interiorization of his concentration lingers, the fact of inner awareness expands. As the experiment is repeated daily, duplicating the same sequence of steps, further awareness of the subject's inner mental states occurs. These repeated experiments yield more knowledge and the eventual power of control over the full range of consciousness.

Through first-hand exposure the experimenter-meditator now knows that he is not his variable, that his identity is more than his thoughts and feelings, that he is more than the customary moods that occupy his normal hours. By investigating meditation, he investigates himself; by investigating himself, he discovers the perdurable factor which not only gives continuity to life's experiences but also remains intact through all personality changes. In the controlled experiment of meditating, the investigator-meditator discovers the substantial constant: the awareness-presence of his self-consciousness.

The meditation experiment is not an isolated event. Samplings of various subject-meditators will concur on similar findings. The experiment of meditation yields not merely private insight but universal knowledge about human nature. With continual experimentations, the investigator-meditator will make further refinements and eventually will discover that this dynamic constant expresses itself in combined variations that account for the personality and attitudinal complexions of people as well as their growth or lagging on the road to adult maturity.

Among investigations into the experiment of meditation, the experimentor will note that the latitude of his mind assumes certain modifications time and time again. The subject chooses to judge and act in certain ways that may not benefit the individual. The mind becomes habituated to certain mental fluctuations – restricting its perception, judging, and responding – without realizing that there is more enrichment to experience. Individuals continue to restrict their options, as it were, by fixed responses to life situations. These habitual rehearsals, the scientist will discover, pave the way to suffering.

Since the mind chooses its irresponsible constraints, a condition must be arranged to recognize these limiting variables. Meditation is the antithesis of an undisciplined mind. The experimenter's steady observation of the active contents of his mind, however, awakens a discernment that allows a release from the binding connection to self-imposed variables. The persistent "witness state" of mind illuminates the inherent difference between the knower and the range of the known variables. Hence dependency on certain ideas and actions are an option, not a moral or compulsive necessity for survival.

Meditation is the experimental science of human consciousness. Everything one does, feels, wishes, or imagines is possible because consciousness is the underlying reality. Meditation is not a science of thinking; the reasoning realm is only one of consciousness' functions or levels. As a process of attending to the interiorization of awareness, meditation has the power to release one's chronic attention to images and ideas. It eventually expands ordinary sensory-bound awareness beyond the margins of rational concepts into the broader regions of creative intuition, exploring the fuller range of consciousness.

Meditation has certain properties and empirical characteristics that are essential to its discoverable nature. These experimental constants emerge during daily tests which vindicate the enterprise: increased tranquility, healthier blood pressure, slower and more stable heart rate, less tension, more relaxed sleep, and the data continues to grow. This substantial body of evidence indicates that the experimenter is proceeding properly.

In scientific journals the abundant articles have shown, for example, that the DHEA hormonal levels of meditators were significantly higher than non-practitioners, thus enabling meditators to concentrate better in all tasks of life. The practice of meditation shows a definite reduction in the release of cortisol, which impairs the function of brain cells. These benefits, along with a return to normal blood pressure and an increase in hemoglobin and lymphocyte counts, reveal the undeniable evidence that meditation improves the blood supply to the brain and enhances metabolism.

The systematic practice of meditation gives one a sense of reassurance that its science is not hit-or-miss. Finally, at the practical, everyday level of jostling with life, one learns through meditation that the seeds of contentment are sown within, and by nourishing them often, a bridge is built to more intelligent living in the outside world.

It's Not
What
You Think!

Imagine putting yourself into a state of mind where there are no mental distractions, no badgering memories, no confused thinking, no hankering desires, no anxieties about the future. Instead, you are left spellbound with a consolidated sense of emotional serenity, clarity of discernment, and quiet bliss that defies rational analysis. What's more, this state abides.

The ancient enlightened ones described this state as *dhyanam nirvishayam manah* – an ineffable, stable liberation from all mental and emotional disturbances. When one arrives at the summit of meditation, known otherwise as *samadhi*, one enters that inner homeland where all questions are finally answered.

In this state you have redefined yourself without depending upon any external resource. You have entered the supernatural realm, the Superconscious state, wherein lies an inexpressible expansion of the personality beyond its confines of body, discursive mind, normal faculties, and egotistical borders. All confines are now broken open. You may return to them any time, but now from the vantage point of transcendence and wisdom.

This sublime goal is not an insult to your trusted rationality. Rather, it's the culmination of your intelligent efforts to grasp the suspected unity of life. To learn about and experience our existence over the years has both rewarded and whetted our appetite for self-knowledge. Yet the uneven path of our cognitive endeavors that prompted so many unanswerable questions has led us to read, speculate, and discuss without satiety. Our enthralling quest to know and experience the fullness of life has led us to a threshold wherein lies, finally, the opportunity to breach the borders of our rational inquiries so as to fathom the mystery of existence. The answer to our aspirations is at hand.

> There is an integrity of self at the very core of your being. It is what gives you your vitality. It can't be lost no matter how you violate your nature. It is recalled fully at the summit of experience.
>
> *George Santayana*

To be in *samadhi* means to dwell in the fountainhead of human existence where no unanswered inquiries remain, where an ambiance of consciousness resides, coeval with your immortal presence and unalloyed bliss. This state places you into the experience of an unprecedented liberty of awareness, suspected by but unknown to your rational cast of mind.

Before, the territory of your life experiences kept you upon the plane of sensible, rational contact with the partial pleasures and recurring sorrows of life. Now, an unbridled magnitude of perception and comprehension occurs that surpasses the limits of reason. You have arrived, as Plato put it, wherein one knows with the knowledge that the gods possess. You, the lover of wisdom, stand at the helm of your destiny.

Imagine, for the moment, what it must be like to cross the empirical confinements of terrestrial time and space and enter at will into a state of existence where there are no secrets and you roam, as it were, expressing choices with incomprehensible emancipation. The indestructible beauty of existence is your cognitive partner forever. The sages referred to this transcendent marvel of human existence as *savikalpa samadhi*.

Yet there is more. Your journey isn't over. Awaiting you is the final silent epiphany of universal existence. You live in such judicious accord with the ultimate state of eternal being that your individuality dissolves into ultimate Oneness. In *nirvikalpa samadhi* the seeker finally merges with the Ideal.

The unbelievable part of this kind of prevailing existence, obscured until now by your pusillanimous avoidance to live a lifestyle consistent with its calling, is that it reveals your natural profile. All the time, but unknown to you, *samadhi* has been your resume. To have known that you possessed unconstrained liberty and boundless access to the actual power to form your exclusive destiny, however, would have emotionally overwhelmed and even terrified your wildest expectations at your egotistical level.

That is why this unsurpassed knowledge, power, and joy demands dues. The final disclosure requires for its full expansion a seasoned maturity of responsible awareness, a demeanor of moral integrity that regards reality as a trust, and a resourceful poise amid the unpredictable flux of daily life.

Here is where meditation-in-action comes into fruition. Students forget that their commitment to medittion, however faltering, involves equally a pledge to live life ingenuously. Exercising these two expressions together forms the daily self-training, "asceticism" as our Greek heritage called it.

To persist in your daily commitment, *sadhana*, to the inner practices, *abhyasa*, with a judicious attitude, *vairagya*, you can't help but transform your character in the direction to which you aspire.

Without a certain ripening over time enabled by the frank facing of one's aspirations, mistakes, flounderings, and recoveries, life repeats its apparent mediocrity for you. Neither God nor genes assembles the threshold of opportunities for growth. You alone become the discerner, the principal agent of constructing the choices for full self-disclosure. You assume authority to confirm your goal because no one else can author it.

An invisible and subtle essence is the Spirit of the whole universe. That is reality. Thou art that.

Chandogya Upanishad

Dr. Justin O'Brien
Swami Jaidev Bharati

Dr. Justin O'Brien
Swami Jaidev Bharati

Justin O'Brien, also known as Swami Jaidev Bharati, is a Renaissance man: philosopher, theologian, yoga practitioner, teacher, writer, wellness expert, speaker, spiritual guide, and long-time explorer in human consciousness.

Known internationally for his programs in spiritual development, wellness, and scholarship, his insights translate across East and West, self-care skills and human development, but always with an emphasis on personal growth. Chief consultant and designer for world conferences on the future of humanity in Tokyo, Kathmandu, New Delhi, Chicago, and New York, he has lectured across the globe, bringing joy and keen insights to many.

He served as Professor of Theology at Loyola University Chicago, Lecturer at the New School for Social Research in New York, and Senior Research Fellow in Holistic Medicine at the University of London. He was Director of Education at the Marylebone Health Centre, London, as well as faculty and Director of Education at the Himalayan International Institute of Yoga Science and Philosophy of USA. He is now Adjunct Professor in the Masters of Liberal Studies Department of the University of Minnesota and preceptor of the Institute of the Himalayan Tradition in Saint Paul, Minnesota.

He has studied theology under the acclaimed

theologians Schillebeeckx, Schoonenberg, and Cooke, holding a Doctorate in the Philosophy of Consciousness and a Doctorate in Theology from Nijmegen University in the Netherlands. He also received a M.A. in Theology from Marquette University, Milwaukee; an M.A. and B.A. in Philosophy from Saint Albert's College, Oakland, California, and a B.A. in the Great Books Classics from the University of Notre Dame. He is also certified in Neurolinguistic Programming and Ericksonian Hypnosis.

O'Brien's life took a giant step into personal growth when he became a disciple of the great yogi, Swami Rama of the Himalayas. He lived, worked, and studied with the saint for twenty-four years, in the States, India, and Nepal. He took spiritual vows in Saint Paul in 1989 and vows of renunciation on the banks of the Ganges River in Rishikesh, India in 1999.

His other books include: *Walking with a Himalayan Master: An American's Odyssey*, *A Meeting of Mystic Paths: Christianity and Yoga*, *The Wellness Tree: The Dynamic Program for Creating Optimal Wellness*, *Running and Breathing*, and *Mirrors for Men*. He is also a contributing author to *Western Spirituality*, *Spirituality for the Religious Educator*, and *Meditation in Christianity*. Several of his books have won national awards, and some of his articles won the NCWA Journalism Award.

Institute of the Himalayan Tradition

The Institute of the Himalayan Tradition was inaugurated as a spiritual educational center by the saint, His Holiness Swami Rama of the Himalayas. Swami Jaidev and Ma Devi, long-time disciples and close companions of Swami Rama, are the spiritual directors of IHT.

They, together with a distinguished faculty, visiting swamis and yogis, certified hatha yoga teachers, health professionals, and dedicated students pass on the ancient wisdom of the Himalayan Sages together with modern science and art in classes, seminars, retreats, initiations, hatha yoga and meditation teacher training, spiritual guidance, and celebrations.

IHT is a forum for those who wish to explore their potential, to reach beyond the obvious, to take another look at themselves, so that we all can reach that which we call the Self.

Throughout the year IHT offers workshops in holistic transformative training that touch our daily lives from the mundane to the sacred, from business to mythology. These classes are taught and facilitated by experienced teachers who have, in turn, been taught by others, and they by others, in a direct line of spiritual teachers reaching back for thousands of years.

We also provide a training center where those who are interested in their personal development may come to learn about and practice the intricacies of the spiritual life, share experiences and ask questions, celebrate the joys, and share in the support of like-minded seekers.

IHT publishes a spiritual magazine, *Himalayan Path*, which contains information on spiritual growth, hatha yoga, yoga psychology and philosophy, meditation, inspiration, the lives of saints, and spiritual practices for the practical world, all in line with the Himalayan Tradition of Yoga. Call, write, or email the office to subscribe.

Institute of the Himalayan Tradition
1317 Summit Avenue, Saint Paul,
MN 55105-2602 651-645-1291
www.ihtyoga.org, info@ihtyoga.org

Full Circle and Hind Pocket Books publish books on inspirational subjects, religion, philosophy, and natural health. The objective is to help make an attitudinal shift towards a more peaceful, loving, non-combative, non-threatening, compassionate and healing world.

We continue our commitment towards creating a peaceful and harmonious world and towards rekindling the joyous, divine nature of the human spirit.

Our fine books are available at all leading bookstores across the country and the Full Circle premium bookstores below:

BOOKSTORES

23, Khan Market, 1st & 2nd Floor
New Delhi-110003 Tel: 24655641/2/3

N-16, Greater Kailash Part I Market
New Delhi-110048 Tel: 29245641/3/4

Number 8, Nizamuddin East Market
New Delhi-110013 Tel: 41826124/5

contact@fullcirclebooks.in
www.fullcirclebooks.in

FullCircle@Chamiers,
New # 106, Chamiers Road
R A Puram, Chennai-600028
Tel: 044-42030733 / 42036833
www.chamiersshop.com

" Dr Frawley provides a dazzling introduction to the world's most enduring meditation tradition.... David Frawley's best book yet."

LINDA JOHNSEN
author of
Meditation is
Boring: Putting Life
in Your Spiritual
Practice

Vedantic Meditation
David Frawley

Vedantic Meditation is 'a must read' for anyone on a spiritual path. It is a pure and authentic depiction of Vedanta.

According to the Vedas, a disconnection of mind and heart leads to all the suffering that we see in the world today. Scientists blame stress for eighty percent of our diseases. This is why, Dr. Frawley points out, having a meditation practice in your life is so important.

You don't have to sit in a cave –
A simple guide to spirituality in daily life.

I consider myself privileged to add a wayfarer's footnote to this remarkable handbook of the spirit made for all of us hitchhiking through the universe.

Paul Zacharia
in a foreword to
Mind the Gap

Mind the Gap
Sukshmananda Swami

A remarkable book for the 21st century. Sukshmananda Swami takes you hitchhiking through the universe, on an exhilarating trip, the destination of which is a place of freedom.

This book takes you easily through the practice of spirituality without making you feel burdened or overwhelmed with complex concepts. Simple and powerful ways to meditate correctly are included. *Mind the Gap* fills you with hope and wisdom.